Small Compline
and
Evening Prayers

According to the usage
of Holy Trinity Monastery
Jordanville, New York

HOLY TRINITY PUBLICATIONS
The Printshop of St Job of Pochaev
Holy Trinity Monastery
Jordanville, New York
2022

Icon of The Most Holy Theotokos, Saver of Souls

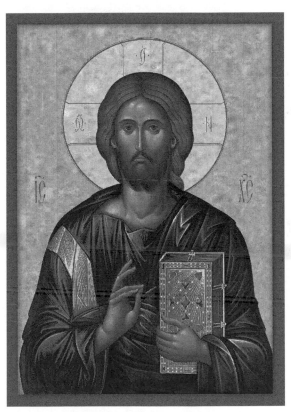

The Pantocrator icon of Christ

Printed with the blessing of
His Eminence, Metropolitan Hilarion,
First Hierarch
of the Russian Orthodox Church Outside of Russia

Third Edition:
Small Compline and Evening Prayers
© 2022 Holy Trinity Monastery
Second Edition text: © 2011 Holy Trinity Monastery
ISBN 978-0-884645-129-1

PSJP
PRINTSHOP OF
SAINT JOB OF POCHAEV

An imprint of:
HOLY TRINITY PUBLICATIONS
Jordanville, New York 13361–0036
www.HolyTrinityPublications.com

ISBN 978-0-884645-487-2 (paperback)

The Psalms taken from: *A Psalter for Prayer*,
trans. David Mitchell James
(Jordanville, NY: Holy Trinity Publications, 2011).

The Order
of
Small Compline
and
Evening Prayers

PRIEST: Blessed is our God, always, now and ever, and unto the ages of ages.

READER: Amen. Glory to Thee, our God, glory to Thee.

O Heavenly King, Comforter, Spirit of Truth, Who art everywhere present and fillest all things, Treasury of good things and Giver of Life: Come and dwell in us, and cleanse us of all impurity, and save our souls, O Good One.

Holy God, Holy Mighty, Holy Immortal, have mercy on us. *Thrice.*

Glory to the Father, and to the Son, and to the Holy Spirit, both now and ever, and unto the ages of ages. Amen.

O Most Holy Trinity, have mercy on us. O Lord, blot out our sins. O Master, pardon our iniquities. O Holy One, visit and heal our infirmities for Thy name's sake.

Lord, have mercy. *Thrice.*

Glory to the Father, and to the Son, and to the Holy Spirit, both now and ever, and unto the ages of ages. Amen.

Our Father, Who art in the heavens, hallowed be Thy name. Thy kingdom come, Thy will be done, on earth as it is in heaven. Give us this day our daily bread, and forgive us our debts, as we forgive our debtors; and lead us not into temptation, but deliver us from the evil one.

PRIEST: For Thine is the kingdom, and the power, and the glory, of the Father, and of the Son, and of the Holy Spirit, now and ever, and unto the ages of ages.

READER: Amen. Lord, have mercy. *Twelve times.*

Glory to the Father, and to the Son, and to the Holy Spirit, both now and ever, and unto the ages of ages. Amen.

O come let us worship God, our King.

O come let us worship and fall down before Christ, our King and God.

O come let us worship and fall down before Christ Himself, our King and God.

Psalm 50

Have mercy upon me, O God, after Thy great goodness, and according to the multitude of Thy mercies do away mine offences. Wash me thoroughly from my wickedness, and cleanse me from my sin. For I know my fault, and my sin is ever before me. Against Thee only have I sinned, and done evil before Thee, that Thou mightest be justified in Thy words, and prevail when Thou art judged. For behold, I was conceived in wickedness, and in sins did my mother bear me. For behold, Thou hast loved truth; the hidden and secret things of Thy wisdom hast Thou revealed unto me. Thou shalt sprinkle me with hyssop, and I shall be made clean; Thou shalt wash me, and I shall become whiter than snow. Thou shalt give joy and gladness to my hearing; the bones that have been humbled will rejoice. Turn Thy face from my sins, and put out all my misdeeds. Make me a clean heart, O God, and renew a right spirit within me. Cast me not away from Thy presence, and take not Thy Holy Spirit from me. O give me the comfort of Thy salvation, and stablish me with Thy governing Spirit. Then shall I teach Thy ways unto the wicked, and the ungodly shall be converted unto Thee. Deliver me from blood-guiltiness, O God, the God of my salvation, and my tongue shall rejoice in Thy righteousness. O Lord, open Thou my lips, and my mouth shall show forth Thy praise. For if Thou hadst desired sacrifice, I would have given it; but Thou delightest not in burnt offerings. The sacrifice unto God is a contrite spirit; a contrite and humble heart God shall not despise. O Lord, be favorable in Thy good will unto Zion, and let the walls of Jerusalem be builded up. Then shalt Thou be pleased with the sacrifice of righteousness, with oblation and whole-burnt offerings; then shall they offer young bullocks upon Thine altar.

Psalm 69

O God, make speed to save me; O Lord, make haste to help me. Let them be ashamed and confounded that seek after my soul. Let them be turned backward and be ashamed that wish me evil. Let them for their reward be soon brought to shame that say over me, Well, well. Let all those that seek Thee be joyful and glad in Thee, O God, and let all such as delight in Thy salvation say always, The Lord be praised. But I am poor and needy, O God; help me! Thou art my helper and my redeemer, O Lord; make no long tarrying.

Psalm 142

O Lord, hear my prayer, consider my supplication in Thy truth; hearken unto me in Thy righteousness, and enter not into judgment with Thy servant, for before Thee shall no man living be justified. For the enemy hath persecuted my soul; he hath smitten my life down to the ground; he hath laid me in the darkness, as those that have been long dead, and my spirit is despondent within me, and my heart within me is vexed. I remembered the days of old; I mused upon all Thy works; I exercised myself in the works of Thy hands. I stretched forth my hands unto Thee; my soul gasped unto Thee as a thirsty land. Hear me soon, O Lord, for my spirit faltereth; turn not Thy face from me, or I shall be like unto them that go down into the pit. O let me hear Thy mercy in the morning, for in Thee have I trusted; tell me, O Lord, the way that I should walk in, for I lift up my soul unto Thee. Deliver me from mine enemies, O Lord, for I have fled unto Thee. Teach me to do Thy will, for Thou art my God. Thy good Spirit shall lead me into the land of righteousness. For Thy Name's sake, O Lord, quicken me by Thy truth; Thou shalt bring my soul out of trouble. And of Thy mercy Thou shalt slay mine enemies, and destroy all them that vex my soul, for I am Thy servant.

Glory to God in the highest, and on earth peace, good will among men. We praise Thee, we bless Thee, we worship Thee, we glorify Thee, we give thanks to Thee for Thy great glory. O Lord, Heavenly King, God the Father Almighty; O Lord, the Only-begotten Son, Jesus Christ; and O Holy Spirit. O Lord God, Lamb of God,

Son of the Father, that takest away the sin of the world, have mercy on us; Thou that takest away the sins of the world, receive our prayer; Thou that sittest at the right hand of the Father, have mercy on us. For Thou only art holy, Thou only art the Lord, Jesus Christ, to the glory of God the Father. Amen.

Every night will I bless Thee, and I will praise Thy name for ever, yea, for ever and ever.

Lord, Thou hast been our refuge in generation and generation. I said: O Lord, have mercy on me, heal my soul, for I have sinned against Thee. O Lord, unto Thee have I fled for refuge, teach me to do Thy will, for Thou art my God. For in Thee is the fountain of life, in Thy light shall we see light. O continue Thy mercy unto them that know Thee.

Vouchsafe, O Lord, to keep us this night without sin. Blessed art Thou, O Lord, the God of our fathers, and praised and glorified is Thy name unto the ages. Amen.

Let Thy mercy, O Lord, be upon us, according as we have hoped in Thee. Blessed art Thou, O Lord, teach me Thy statutes. Blessed art Thou, O Master, give me understanding of Thy statutes. Blessed art Thou, O Holy One, enlighten me by Thy statutes.

O Lord, Thy mercy endureth for ever; disdain not the work of Thy hands. To Thee is due praise, to Thee is due a song; to Thee glory is due, to the Father, and to the Son, and to the Holy Spirit, now and ever, and unto the ages of ages. Amen.

I believe in one God, the Father Almighty, Maker of heaven and earth and of all things visible and invisible. And in one Lord Jesus Christ, the Son of God, the Only-begotten, begotten of the Father before all ages. Light of Light, True God of True God; begotten, not made; of one essence with the Father, by Whom all things were made. Who for us men and for our salvation, came down from the heavens, and was incarnate of the Holy Spirit and the Virgin Mary, and became man; and was crucified for us under Pontius Pilate, and suffered, and was buried; And arose on the third day according to the Scriptures; and ascended into the heavens and sitteth at the right hand of the Father; and shall come again, with glory, to judge both the living and the dead; Whose kingdom shall have no end. And in the Holy Spirit, the Lord, the Giver of Life; Who proceedeth from the Father; Who with the Father and the Son together is worshipped and glorified; Who spake by the prophets. In One Holy, Catholic and Apostolic Church. I confess one baptism for the remission of sins. I look for the resurrection of the dead, and the life of the age to come. Amen.

After this, we sing a canon from the Menaion, or from the Octoechos. And after the canon (and stichera), we chant:

It is truly meet to bless Thee, the Theotokos, ever-blessed and most blameless, and Mother of our God. More honorable than the Cherubim, and beyond compare more glorious than the Seraphim, who without corruption gavest birth to God the Word, the very Theotokos, thee do we magnify.

READER: Holy God, Holy Mighty, Holy Immortal, have mercy on us. *Thrice.*

Glory to the Father, and to the Son, and to the Holy Spirit, both now and ever, and unto the ages of ages. Amen.

O Most Holy Trinity, have mercy on us. O Lord, blot out our sins. O Master, pardon our iniquities. O Holy One, visit and heal our infirmities for Thy name's sake.

Lord, have mercy. *Thrice.*

Glory to the Father, and to the Son, and to the Holy Spirit, both now and ever, and unto the ages of ages. Amen.

Our Father, Who art in the heavens, hallowed be Thy name. Thy kingdom come, Thy will be done, on earth as it is in heaven. Give us this day our daily bread, and forgive us our debts, as we forgive our debtors; and lead us not into temptation, but deliver us from the evil one.

PRIEST: For Thine is the kingdom, and the power, and the glory, of the Father, and of the Son, and of the Holy Spirit, now and ever, and unto the ages of ages.

READER: Amen.

———

*Then, if it be a **forefeast** or an **afterfeast**, he reads its kontakion followed immediately by "Lord, have mercy" forty times and the rest: see page 25.*

*But if it be a **simple weekday service**, he reads the appointed troparia. If the **temple be dedicated to the Saviour or to the Mother of God**, then first we say the troparion of the temple, then the troparion of the*

day (see below), then O God of our fathers
... and so forth: see page 22.

If the **temple be dedicated to a saint**,
*the troparion of the day is said first, then
the troparion of the temple, then* "Lord,
have mercy" *forty times and the rest:
see page 25.*

On Sunday night:

Supreme commanders of the heavenly
hosts, we unworthy ones implore you
that by your supplications ye will encircle
us with the shelter of the wings of your
immaterial glory, and guard us who fall
down before you and fervently cry: Deliver
us from dangers since ye are the marshalls
of the hosts on high.

On Monday night:

The memory of the Righteous is celebrated with hymns of praise, but the Lord's testimony is sufficient for thee, O Forerunner; for thou hast proved to be truly even more venerable than the Prophets since thou wast granted to baptize in the running waters Him Whom they proclaimed. Wherefore, having contested for the truth, thou didst rejoice to announce the good tidings even to those in hades; that God hath appeared in the flesh, taking away the sin of the world and granting us great mercy.

On Tuesday night:

Save, O Lord, Thy people, and bless Thine inheritance; grant Thou victory to Orthodox Christians over enemies; and by the power of Thy Cross do Thou preserve Thy commonwealth.

On Wednesday night:

O holy apostles, intercede with the merciful God, that He grant unto our souls forgiveness of offenses.

And the Troparion to Saint Nicholas:

The truth of things revealed thee to thy flock as a rule of faith, an icon of meekness and a teacher of temperance; therefore, thou hast achieved the heights by humility, riches by poverty. O Father and Hierarch Nicholas, intercede with Christ God that our souls be saved.

On Thursday night:

Save, O Lord, Thy people, and bless Thine inheritance; grant Thou victory to

Orthodox Christians over enemies; and by the power of Thy Cross do Thou preserve Thy commonwealth.

Then, Sunday night through Thursday night:

O God of our fathers, Who ever dealest by us according to Thy kindness, take not Thy mercy from us, but through their intercessions guide our life in peace.

Adorned in the blood of Thy martyrs throughout all the world, as in purple and fine linen, Thy Church, through them doth cry unto Thee, O Christ God: Send down Thy compassions upon Thy people; grant peace to Thy flock, and to our souls great mercy.

Glory to the Father, and to the Son, and to the Holy Spirit.

With the saints give rest, O Christ, to the souls of Thy servants, where there is neither sickness, nor sorrow, nor sighing, but life everlasting.

Both now and ever, and unto the ages of ages. Amen.

Through the intercessions, O Lord, of all the saints and the Theotokos, grant us Thy peace, and have mercy on us, as Thou alone art compassionate.

But on Friday night:

O apostles, martyrs, and prophets, hierarchs, monastics, and righteous ones; ye who have accomplished a good labor and kept the faith, who have boldness before the Saviour; O good ones, intercede for us, we pray, that our souls be saved.

Glory to the Father, and to the Son, and to the Holy Spirit.

With the saints give rest, O Christ, to the souls of Thy servants, where there is neither sickness, nor sorrow, nor sighing, but life everlasting.

Both now and ever, and unto the ages of ages. Amen.

To Thee, O Lord, the Planter of creation, the world doth offer the Godbearing martyrs as the first-fruits of nature. By their intercessions preserve Thy Church, Thy commonwealth, in profound peace, through the Theotokos, O Greatly merciful One.

On Saturday at Small Compline, *we read the Resurrectional troparion and kontakion in the tone of the week.*

Then: Lord, have mercy. *Forty times.*

Thou Who at all times and at every hour, in heaven and on earth, art worshipped and glorified, O Christ God, Who art long-suffering, plenteous in mercy, most compassionate, Who lovest the righteous and hast mercy on sinners, Who callest all to salvation through the promise of good things to come: Receive, O Lord, our prayers at this hour, and guide our life toward Thy commandments. Sanctify our souls, make chaste our bodies, correct our thoughts, purify our intentions, and deliver us from every sorrow, evil, and pain. Compass us about with Thy holy angels; that, guarded and guided by their array, we may attain to the unity of the faith and the knowledge of Thine unapproachable glory; for blessed art Thou unto the ages of ages. Amen.

Lord, have mercy. *Thrice.*

Glory to the Father, and to the Son, and to the Holy Spirit, both now and ever, and unto the ages of ages. Amen.

More honorable than the Cherubim, and beyond compare more glorious than the Seraphim, Who without corruption gavest birth to God the Word, the very Theotokos, Thee do we magnify.

In the name of the Lord, father, bless.

PRIEST: Through the prayers of our holy fathers, O Lord Jesus Christ our God, have mercy on us.

READER: Amen.

IN LENT

*On Sunday nights of Great Lent, the **Prayer of St Ephraim the Syrian** is said here, including the 12 bows.*

O Lord and Master of my life, give me not a spirit of idleness, despondency, ambition and idle talking. *Prostration.*

But rather a spirit of chastity, humble-mindedness, patience, and love bestow upon me Thy servant. *Prostration.*

Yea, O Lord King, grant me to see my failings and not condemn my brother; for blessed art Thou unto the ages of ages. Amen. *Prostration.*

O God, cleanse me a sinner. *Twelve times, with a reverence each time.*

Then: Holy God… Our Father…

PRIEST: For Thine is the kingdom…

READER: Amen. Lord, have mercy. *Twelve times.*

Then:

O undefiled, untainted, uncorrupted, most pure, chaste Virgin, Thou Bride of God and Sovereign Lady, Who didst unite the Word of God unto mankind through Thy most glorious birthgiving, and hast linked the apostate nature of our race with the heavenly; Who art the only hope of the hopeless, and the helper of the struggling, the ever-ready protection of them that hasten unto Thee, and the refuge of all Christians: Do not shrink with loathing from me, a sinner defiled, who with polluted thoughts, words, and deeds have made myself utterly unprofitable, and through slothfulness of mind have become a slave to the pleasures of life. But as the Mother of God Who loveth mankind, show Thy love for mankind and mercifully have compassion upon me a sinner and prodigal, and accept my supplication, which is offered to Thee out of my defiled mouth; and making use of Thy motherly boldness, entreat Thy Son and our Master and Lord that He may be pleased to open for me the bowels of His loving-kindness and graciousness to mankind, and, disregarding my numberless offenses, will turn me back to repentance and show me to be a tried worker of His precepts. And be Thou ever present unto me as merciful, compassionate, and well-disposed; in the present life, be Thou a fervent intercessor and helper, repelling the assaults of adversaries and guiding me to salvation, and at the time of my departure, taking care of my miserable soul, and driving far away from it the dark countenances of evil demons; lastly, at the dreadful day of judgment delivering me from torment eternal and showing me to be an heir of the ineffable glory of Thy Son and our God; all of which may I attain, O my Sovereign Lady, most holy Theotokos, in virtue of Thine intercession and protection, through the grace and love to mankind of Thine Only-begotten Son, our Lord and God and Saviour, Jesus Christ; to Whom is due all glory, honor, and worship, together with His Unoriginate Father, and His Most-holy and good and life-creating Spirit, now and ever, and unto the ages of ages. Amen.

And this Prayer, to our Lord Jesus Christ:

And grant unto us, O Master, in the coming sleep, rest for soul and body, and preserve us from the gloomy slumber of sin, and from every dark and nocturnal sensuality. Subdue the impulses of passions, quench the fiery darts of the evil one that are cunningly hurled against us, assuage the rebellions of our flesh, and every earthly and fleshly subtlety of ours lull to sleep. And grant unto us, O God, a watchful mind, chaste thought, a sober heart, a sleep gentle and free from every satanic illusion. Raise us up at the time of prayer firmly grounded in Thy precepts, and keeping steadfastly within us the memory of Thy judgments. All the night long grant us a doxology; that we may hymn and bless and glorify Thy most honorable and majestic name: of the Father, and of the Son, and of the Holy Spirit, now and ever, and unto the ages of ages. Amen.

In Lent

On Sunday evenings of Great Lent, we begin immediately the "Prayers on Approaching Sleep," *see page 34.*

Outside Great Lent, these troparia are said.

Sixth Tone:

Have mercy on us, O Lord, have mercy on us; for at a loss for any defense, this prayer do we sinners offer unto Thee as Master: have mercy on us.

Glory to the Father, and to the Son, and to the Holy Spirit.

Lord, have mercy on us; for we have hoped in Thee, be not angry with us greatly, neither remember our iniquities; but look upon us now as Thou art compassionate, and deliver us from our enemies; for Thou art our God, and we, Thy people, all are the works of Thy hands, and we call upon Thy name.

Both now and ever,…

Theotokion: The door of compassion open unto us, O blessed Theotokos, for, hoping in Thee, let us not perish; through Thee may we be delivered from adversities, for Thou art the salvation of the Christian race.

READER: Lord, have mercy. *Twelve times.*

Prayers on Approaching Sleep

Prayer 1
of St Macarius the Great

O Eternal God and King of all creation, Who hast vouchsafed me to arrive at this hour, forgive me the sins that I have committed this day in deed, word, and thought; and cleanse, O Lord, my lowly soul of all defilement of flesh and spirit; and grant me, O Lord, to pass the sleep of this night in peace; that, rising from my lowly bed, I may please Thy most holy name all the days of my life, and thwart the enemies, fleshly and bodiless, that war against me. And deliver me, O Lord, from vain thoughts and evil desires which defile me. For Thine is the kingdom, and the power, and the glory, of the Father, and of the Son, and of the Holy Spirit, now and ever, and unto the ages of ages. Amen.

Prayer 2,
of St Antiochus

ORuler of all, Word of the Father, O Jesus Christ, Thou Who art perfect: For the sake of the plenitude of Thy mercy, never depart from me, but always abide in me Thy servant. O Jesus, Good Shepherd of Thy sheep, deliver me not over to the sedition of the serpent, and leave me not to the will of Satan, for the seed of corruption is in me. But do Thou, O Lord, worshipful God, holy King, Jesus Christ, as I sleep, guard me by the Unwaning Light, Thy Holy Spirit, by Whom Thou didst sanctify Thy disciples. O Lord, grant me, Thine unworthy servant, Thy salvation upon my bed. Enlighten my mind with the light of

understanding of Thy Holy Gospel; my
soul with the love of Thy Cross; my heart
with the purity of Thy word; my body with
Thy passionless Passion. Keep my thought
in Thy humility, and raise me up at the
proper time for Thy glorification. For most
glorified art Thou together with Thine unoriginate Father, and the Most-holy Spirit,
unto the ages of ages. Amen.

Prayer 3,
to the Holy Spirit

O Lord, Heavenly King, Comforter,
Spirit of Truth, show compassion and
have mercy on me, Thy sinful servant, and
loose me from mine unworthiness, and
forgive all wherein I have sinned against
Thee today as a man, but even worse
than a man, as a beast; my sins voluntary
and involuntary, known and unknown,

whether from youth and from evil sug-
gestion, or whether from brazenness
and despondency. If I have sworn by Thy
name, or blasphemed it in my thought; or
reproached anyone, or slandered anyone
in mine anger, or grieved anyone, or have
become angry about anything; or have lied,
or slept needlessly, or if a beggar hath come
to me and I disdained him; or if I have
grieved my brother, or have quarreled, or
have condemned anyone; or if I have been
boastful, or prideful, or angry; if, as I stood
at prayer, my mind hath been distracted
by the wiles of this world, or by thoughts
of depravity; if I have overeaten, or have
drunk excessively, or laughed frivolously;
if I have thought evil, or seen the beauty
of another and been wounded thereby in
my heart; if I have said improper things, or
derided my brother's sin when mine own

sins are countless; if I have been neglectful of prayer, or have done some other wrong that I do not remember, for all of this and more than this have I done: Have mercy, O Master my Creator, on me Thy downcast and unworthy servant, and loose me, and remit, and forgive me; for Thou art good and the Lover of mankind, so that, lustful, sinful, and wretched as I am, I may lie down and sleep and rest in peace. And I shall worship, and hymn, and glorify Thy most honorable name, together with the Father and His Only-begotten Son, now and ever, and unto the ages of ages. Amen.

Prayer 4,
of St Macarius the Great

What shall I offer Thee, or what shall I give Thee, O greatly-gifted, immortal King, O compassionate Lord Who lovest mankind? For though I have been slothful in pleasing Thee, and have done nothing good, Thou hast led me to the close of this day that is past, establishing the conversion and salvation of my soul. Be merciful to me, a sinner, bereft of every good deed; raise up my fallen soul, which hath become defiled by countless sins, and take away from me every evil thought of this visible life. Forgive my sins, O Only Sinless One, in which I have sinned against Thee this day, known or unknown, in word, and deed, and thought, and in all my senses. Do Thou Thyself protect and guard me from every opposing circumstance, by Thy Divine authority and power and inexpressible love for mankind. Blot out, O God, blot out the multitude of my sins. Be pleased, O Lord, to deliver me from the net of the evil one, and save my passionate soul, and overshadow me with the light of Thy countenance when Thou shalt come in glory; and cause me, uncondemned now, to sleep a dreamless sleep, and keep Thy servant untroubled by thoughts, and drive away from me all satanic deeds; and enlighten for me the eyes of my heart with understanding, lest I sleep unto death. And send me an angel of peace, a guardian and guide of my soul and body, that he may deliver me from mine enemies; that, rising from my bed, I may offer Thee prayers of thanksgiving. Yea, O Lord, hearken unto me, Thy sinful and wretched servant, in confession and conscience; grant me, when I arise, to be instructed by Thy sayings; and through Thine angels cause demonic despondency to be driven far from me: that I may bless Thy holy name, and glorify and extol the most pure Theotokos Mary, whom Thou hast given to us sinners as a protectress, and accept Her who prayeth for us. For I know that She exemplifieth Thy love for mankind and prayeth for us without ceasing. Through Her protection, and the sign of the precious Cross, and for the sake of all Thy saints, preserve my wretched soul, O Jesus Christ our God: for holy art Thou, and most glorious forever. Amen.

Prayer 5

O Lord our God, as Thou art good and the Lover of mankind, forgive me wherein I have sinned today in word, deed, and thought. Grant me peaceful and undisturbed sleep; send Thy guardian angel to protect and keep me from all evil. For Thou art the Guardian of our souls and bodies, and unto Thee do we send up glory: to the

Father, and to the Son, and to the Holy Spirit, now and ever, and unto the ages of ages. Amen.

Prayer 6

O Lord our God, in Whom we believe and Whose Name we invoke above every name, grant us, as we go to sleep, relaxation of soul and body, and keep us from all dreams and dark pleasures; stop the onslaught of the passions and quench the burnings that arise in the flesh. Grant us to live chastely in deed and word, that we may obtain a virtuous life, and not fall away from Thy promised blessings; for blessed art Thou forever. Amen.

Prayer 7,
of St John Chrysostom

(A prayer for each hour of the day and night.)

O Lord, deprive me not of Thy heavenly good things. O Lord, deliver me from the eternal torments. O Lord, if I have sinned in mind or thought, in word or deed, forgive me. O Lord, deliver me from all ignorance, forgetfulness, faintheartedness, and stony insensibility. O Lord, deliver me from every temptation. O Lord, enlighten my heart, which evil desire hath darkened. O Lord, as a man, I have sinned; but do Thou, as the compassionate God, have mercy on me, seeing the infirmity of my soul. O Lord, send Thy grace to my help, that I may glorify Thy holy name. O Lord Jesus Christ, write me, Thy servant, in the Book of Life, and grant me a good end.

O Lord my God, even though I have done nothing good in Thy sight, yet grant me by Thy grace to make a good beginning. O Lord, sprinkle into my heart the dew of Thy grace. O Lord of heaven and earth, remember me, Thy sinful servant, shameful and unclean, in Thy kingdom. Amen.

O Lord, accept me in repentence. O Lord, forsake me not. O Lord, lead me not into temptation. O Lord, grant me good thoughts. O Lord, grant me tears, and remembrance of death, and compunction. O Lord, grant me the thought of confessing my sins. O Lord, grant me humility, chastity, and obedience. O Lord, grant me patience, courage, and meekness. O Lord, implant in me the root of good, fear of Thee in my heart. O Lord, vouchsafe me to love Thee with all my soul and thoughts, and in all things to do Thy will. O Lord, protect me from evil men, and demons, and passions, and from every other unseemly thing. O Lord, Thou knowest that Thou doest as Thou wilt: Thy will be done also in me a sinner; for blessed art Thou unto the ages of ages. Amen.

Prayer 8,
to Our Lord Jesus Christ

O Lord Jesus Christ, Son of God, for the sake of Thy most honorable Mother, and Thy bodiless angels, Thy Prophet and Forerunner and Baptist, the God-inspired apostles, the radiant and victorious martyrs, the holy and God-bearing fathers, and through the intercessions of all the saints, deliver me from the besetting presence of the demons. Yea, my Lord and Creator, Who desirest not the death of a sinner, but rather that he be converted and live, grant conversion also to me, wretched and unworthy; rescue me from the mouth of the pernicious serpent, who is ravening to devour me and drag me down to hell alive. Yea, my Lord, my Comfort, Who for my miserable sake wast clothed in corruptible flesh, draw me out of misery, and grant comfort to my miserable soul. Implant in my heart to fulfill Thy commandments, and to forsake evil deeds, and to obtain Thy blessings; for in Thee, O Lord, have I hoped, save me. Amen.

Prayer 9,
to the Most Holy Theotokos

O Good Mother of the Good King, Most Pure and Blessed Theotokos Mary, do Thou pour out the mercy of Thy Son and our God upon my passionate soul, and by Thine intercessions guide me unto good works, that I may pass the remaining time of my life without defilement, and attain paradise through Thee, O Virgin Theotokos, Who art pure and blessed.

Prayer 10,
to the Holy Guardian Angel

O angel of Christ, my holy guardian and protector of my soul and body, forgive me all wherein I have sinned this day, and deliver me from all the wickedness of mine enemy against me, lest I anger my God by any sin. Pray for me, a sinful and unworthy servant, that thou mayest show me forth worthy of the kindness and mercy of the All-holy Trinity, and of the Mother of my Lord Jesus Christ, and of all the saints. Amen.

Kontakion to the Theotokos:

To Thee, the Champion Leader, we, Thy servants, dedicate a feast of victory and of thanksgiving as ones rescued out of sufferings, O Theotokos; but as Thou art one with might which is invincible, from all dangers that can be do Thou deliver us, that we may cry to Thee: Rejoice, Thou Bride Unwedded!

Most glorious, Ever-Virgin, Mother of Christ God, present our prayer to Thy Son and our God, that through Thee He may save our souls.

All my hope I place in Thee, O Mother of God: keep me under Thy protection.

O Virgin Theotokos, disdain not me a sinner, needing Thy help and Thy protection, and have mercy on me, for my soul hath hoped in Thee.

My hope is the Father; my refuge is the Son; my protection is the Holy Spirit: O Holy Trinity, glory to Thee.

PRIEST: Glory to Thee, O Christ God, our hope, glory to Thee.

CHANTERS: Glory to the Father, and to the Son, and to the Holy Spirit, both now and ever, and unto the ages of ages. Amen.

Lord, have mercy. *Thrice.*

Father, bless.

PRIEST: May Christ our True God, through the intercessions of His most pure Mother, of (*here the saint of the temple is commemorated*) and of all the saints, have mercy on us and save us, for He is good and the Lover of mankind.

CHANTERS: Amen.

PRIEST: Bless, holy fathers and brethren, and forgive me a sinner, all wherein I have sinned this day in deed, word, and thought, and in all my senses.

And we reply: May God forgive and have mercy on thee, holy father.

And we make a bow (or prostration, as the Typicon may require), asking this forgiveness:

Bless me, holy father, and forgive all wherein I have sinned this day in deed, word, and thought, and in all my senses, and pray for me, a sinner.

PRIEST: Through His grace, may God forgive and have mercy on us all.

And he says this litany, while the chanters repeat Lord, have mercy *continuously until the end*:

Again we pray for our great lord and father, the Most Holy Patriarch *N.*; for our lord, the Very Most Reverend Metropolitan *N.*, First Hierarch of the Russian Church Abroad; for our lord the Most Reverend Archbishop [or Bishop] N. *(whose diocese it is),* and for all our brethren in Christ.

For this land, its authoritites, and armed forces, and all who with faith and piety dwell therein, let us pray to the Lord.

For the God-preserved Russian land and its Orthodox people both in the homeland

and in the diaspora, and for their salvation,
let us pray to the Lord.

For them that hate us and them that
love us.

For them that are kind to us and them
that serve us.

For them that have asked us unworthy
ones to pray for them.

For the deliverance of those in captivity.

For our fathers and brethren that
are traveling.

For them that sail upon the sea.

For them that are bedridden
in infirmities.

Let us pray for the abundance of the
fruits of the earth.

And for every Orthodox Christian soul.

Let us bless pious rulers.

Orthodox hierarchs and the founders of this holy monastery.

Our parents and all that have passed on before us, our fathers and brethren, and the Orthodox here and everywhere laid to rest.

Let us say also for ourselves.

CHANTERS: Lord, have mercy. *Thrice.*

PRIEST: For the sake of the intercessions of Thy most pure Mother, of (*the saint of the temple is commemorated here*) and of all the saints, O Lord Jesus Christ our God, have mercy on us.

CHANTERS: Amen. *And we begin to chant the stichera to the Cross (unless it be a fore-*

feast or afterfeast, in which case the proper troparion is chanted instead) as we venerate the holy icons:

Sixth Tone: Being protected by the Cross, we struggle against the enemy, not fearing his deceit and cunning, for the proud one was destroyed and was trampled down by the power of Christ crucified on the Tree.

Thy Cross, O Lord, is sanctified, for by It healings are accomplished for them that are ill with sin; wherefore, we fall down before Thee, have mercy on us.

Eighth Tone: O Lord, a weapon against the devil hast Thou given us in Thy Cross, for he quaketh and trembleth, unable to bear the sight of Its power, for It raiseth the dead, and hath abolished death; therefore we worship Thy burial and arising.

Then we invoke the mercy of God and the intercessions of a litany of locally vener- ated saints as we continue to venerate the Holy icons.

At Holy Trinity Monastery, the litany is chanted as follows:

O Most Holy Trinity, our God, glory to Thee.

Glory, O Lord, to Thy precious Cross and Resurrection.

O most holy Theotokos, save us.

All ye Heavenly Hosts of holy Angels and Archangels, pray to God for us.

O holy Great John, the Forerunner of the Lord, pray to God for us.

Holy Apostle Andrew, pray to God for us.

Holy Apostle and Evangelist Luke, pray to God for us.

Holy Hierarch Abercius,[1] pray to God for us.

Holy Hierarch Nicholas,[2] pray to God for us.

Holy Hierarch Athanasius,[3] pray to God for us.

Holy Hierarchs of Christ, Basil the Great, Gregory the Theologian, and John Chrysostom, pray to God for us.

---

1   St Abercius (Averky) of Hierapolis
2   St Nicholas of Myra in Lycia
3   St Athanasius of Alexandria

Holy Hierarch Mark,[4] pray to God for us.

Holy Hierarch Arsenius,[5] pray to God for us.

Holy Hierarchs of Christ, Mitrophan, Theodosy, and Joasaph,[6] pray to God for us.

Holy Hieromartyrs Dionysius and Haralampus,[7] pray to God for us.

Holy Greatmartyr and Trophybearer George, pray to God for us.

Holy Greatmartyr Demetrius, pray to God for us.

---

4   St Mark of Ephesus
5   St Arsenius of Serbia
6   Sts Mitrophan of Voronezh, Theodosy of Chernigov, and Joasaph of Belgorod
7   Sts Dionysius the Aeropagite and Haralampus

Holy Greatmartyr and Healer Panteleimon, pray to God for us.

Holy Martyr Tryphon,[8] pray to God for us.

Holy Martyr Vitalis, pray to God for us.

Holy Martyr Phanurius,[9] pray to God for us.

Venerable Martyrs of Zographou, pray to God for us.

Holy Great-martyr Barbara, pray to God for us.

Holy Martyr Parasceva, pray to God for us.

Our venerable Father Job,[10] pray to God for us.

8   St Tryphon the Gooseherd
9   St Phanurius of Rhodes
10   St Job of Pochaev

Our venerable Fathers Anthony and Theodosius and the Other Wonderworkers of the Caves, pray to God for us.

Venerable Father Sergius,[11] pray to God for us.

Venerable Father Seraphim,[12] pray to God for us.

Venerable Father John,[13] pray to God for us.

Holy Righteous Caesarius,[14] pray to God for us.

Holy Equal-of-the-Apostles Great Prince Vladimir, pray to God for us.

---

11 St Sergius of Radonezh
12 St Seraphim of Sarov
13 St John of Rila
14 St Caesarius, brother of Gregory the Theologian

Holy Righteous Father John,[15] pray to God for us.

Venerable Father Herman,[16] pray to God for us.

Venerable Father Paisius,[17] pray to God for us.

Venerable Fathers of Optina, pray to God for us.

Holy Blessed Xenia,[18] pray to God for us.

Holy Hierarch Father John,[19] pray to God for us.

O ye New Martyrs and Confessors of Russia, pray to God for us.

---

15 St John of Kronstadt
16 St Herman of Alaska
17 St Paisius Velichkovsky
18 St Xenia of Petersburg
19 St John of Shanghai and San Francisco

All ye Saints of the Russian Land, pray to God for us.

All ye Saints, pray to God for us.

Then the troparion of Pentecost (except during other feasts of the Lord), Eighth Tone:

Blessed art Thou, O Christ our God, Who hast shown forth the fishermen as supremely wise, by sending down upon them the Holy Spirit, and through them didst draw the world into Thy net. O Lover of mankind, glory be to Thee.

Glory to the Father, and to the Son, and to the Holy Spirit.

Troparion to Saint Job of Pochaev, Fourth Tone:

Having acquired the patience of thy longsuffering forefather, and having resembled the Baptist in abstinence, and having shared the divine zeal of both, thou wast vouchsafed worthy to receive their names, and thou wast a fearless preacher of the true Faith. In this way, thou didst bring a multitude of monastics to Christ, and thou didst strengthen all the people in Orthodoxy. O Job our holy father, pray that our souls be saved.

Both now and ever, and unto the ages of ages. Amen.

Troparion to the Pochaev Icon of the Theotokos (except during feasts of the Lord and the Theotokos, when the festal kontakion is chanted instead), Fifth Tone, special melody:

Before Thy holy icon, O Sovereign Lady, they that pray are deemed worthy of healing, receive understanding of the true Faith, and repel the attacks of the Hagarenes. Likewise for us, who fall down before Thee: do Thou ask for forgiveness of our sins. With devout purpose enlighten our hearts, and to Thy Son, raise up Thy prayer for our souls' salvation.

In other churches, troparia for the temple feast, saint, or icon may replace those above.

Then the priest maketh the dismissal:

For the sake of the intercessions of Thy most pure Mother, of our venerable and God-bearing Father Job, Abbot and Wonderworker of Pochaev, and of all the saints, O Lord Jesus Christ our God, have mercy on us.

CHANTERS/PEOPLE: Amen.

THE END OF SMALL COMPLINE